• Alex Brychta and Margaret Grieveson •

At Home with
Oxford Reading Tree

D1739610

Seasons Book

• Oxford University Press •

January

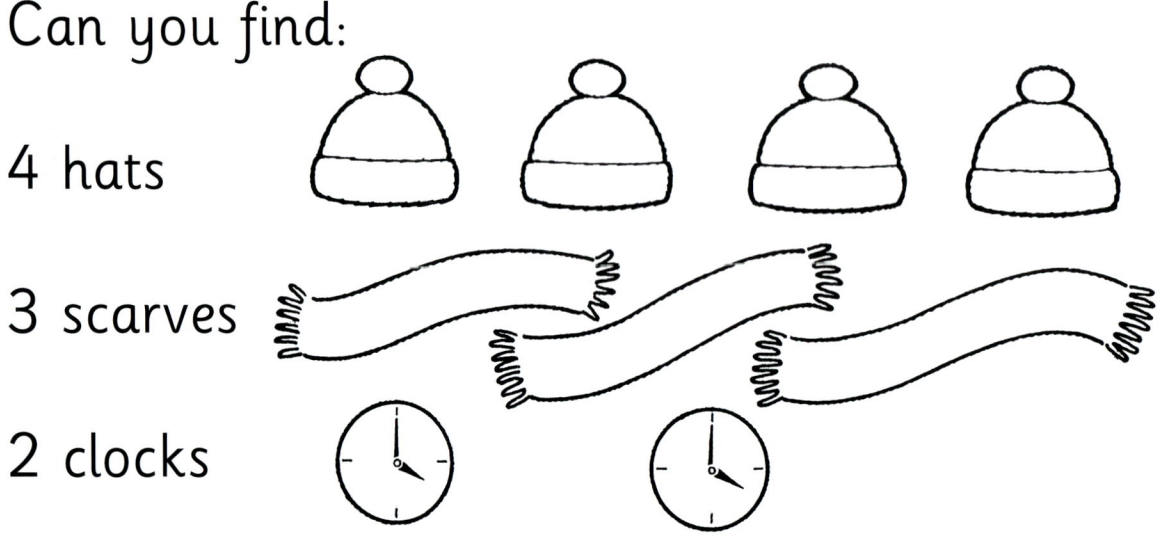

Can you find:

4 hats

3 scarves

2 clocks

Colour them to match the picture.

In January, it snows.

Who is this?

Join the dots.

February

In February, hedgehogs wake up from their winter sleep.

Make a veg hog.

Use mashed potato, carrot sticks, and 3 peas.

March

In March, it is Mother's Day.

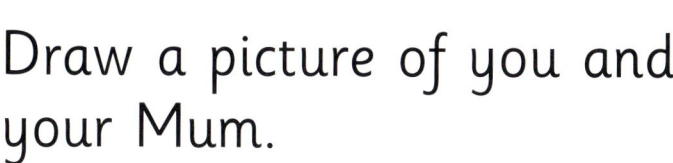

Draw a picture of you and your Mum.

April

Can you find:

a stool

a dustbin

some bricks

a box

In April, we play outside.

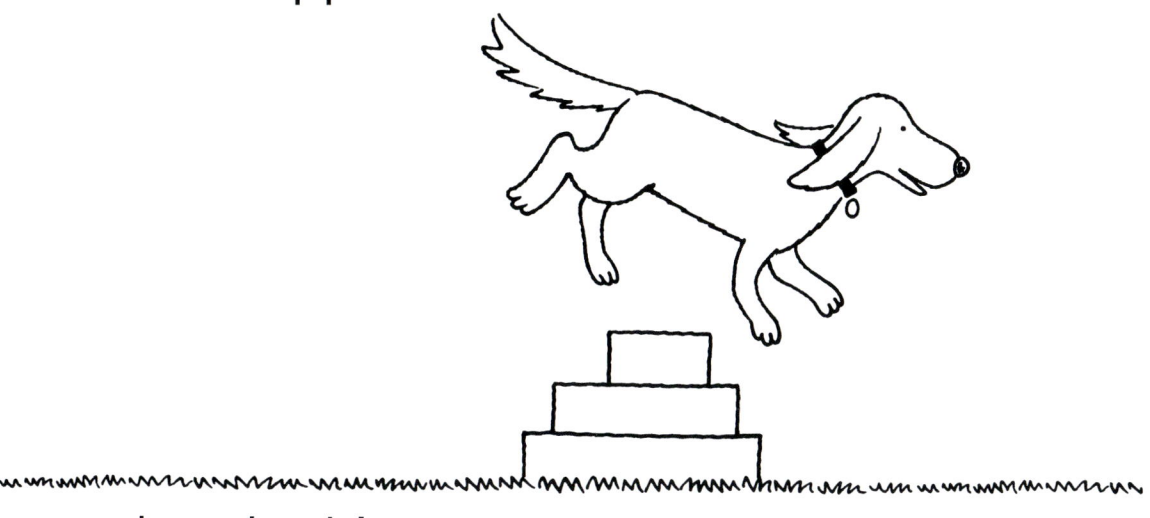

What will happen next?

Draw the plank!

May

What have they found?

Tick or cross.

 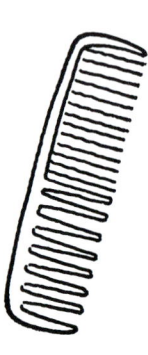  

8

In May, we go to the sea.

Draw the missing parts:

spade   bucket   ice-cream   net

June

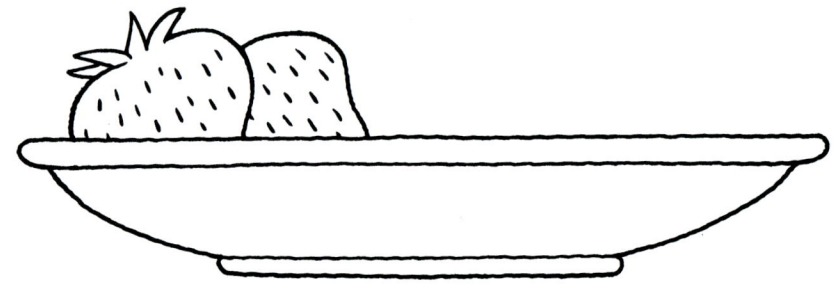

In June, we pick fruit.

Draw more fruit in the fruit bowl.

Match the fruit:

Make a mobile:

Draw, colour, and cut out the fruit shapes.

Hang them on string from a stick.

July

What is in the treasure chest?

Tick or cross.

In July, we go swimming.

Colour the fish.

Give each one a different pattern.

August

Which things make you cool?

Tick or cross.

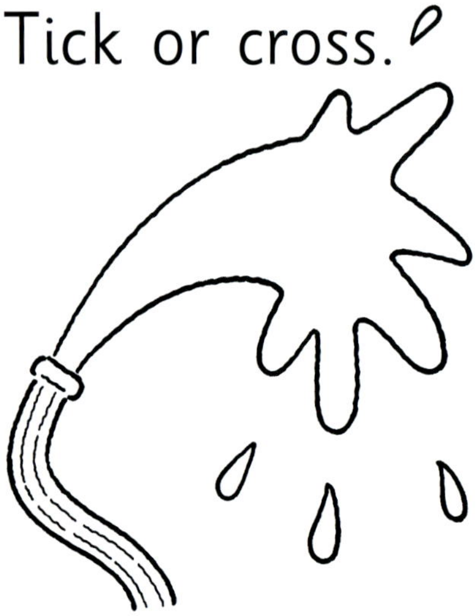

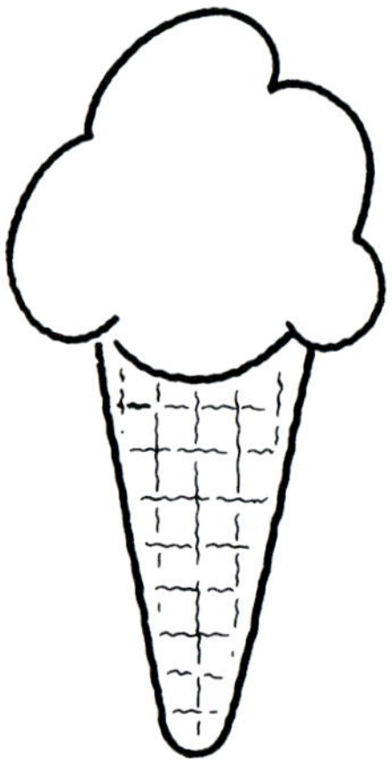

In August, it's hot!

Why is it hot?

Join the dots.

September

Which toy do you like to play with?

Draw it here.

In September, we start school.

What toy is this?

Join the dots.

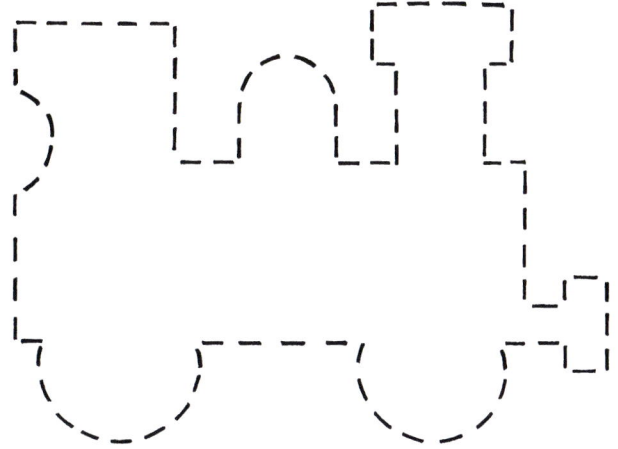

October

Can you find:

a football   a book

a saucepan

Colour them to match the picture.

In October, it is Book Week.

Make a caterpillar to eat.

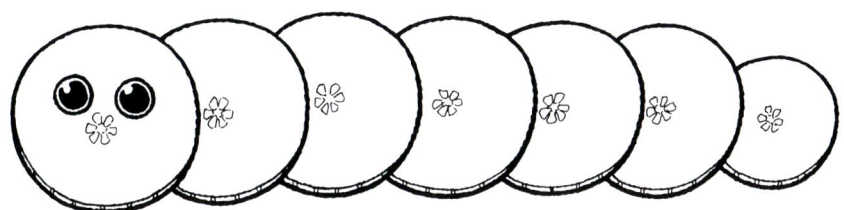

Use cucumber, and raisins.

November

Find a pair of:

boots

hats

glasses

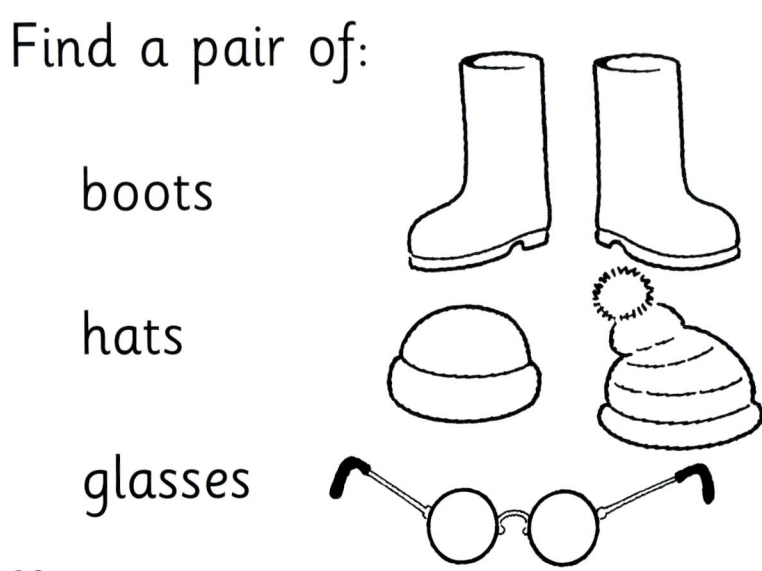

In November, it's windy.

Match the weather:

December

How many:

rats

windows

glasses

In December, it is the school play.

Can you tell these stories:

3 blind mice

3 bears

3 billy goats gruff

Note to parents

This *Seasons Book* will help your child become aware of the pattern of the seasons as they unfold month-by-month through the year. This will lead to learning about concepts of time and weather, and also learning general skills of observation and association.

The activities on each page develop skills of perception and matching, usually reinforced by a suggestion for drawing or making.

The whole series of workbooks is intended to help your child work towards Level 1 of the National Curriculum, through the motivation of the well-known Oxford Reading Tree characters, and the practice of basic pre-reading and writing skills.

Sources

The colour pictures are all reproduced from stories in the Oxford Reading Tree series:

January *Village in the snow*, Stage 5

February *The hedgehog*, Stage 1

March *Poor old Mum*, Stage 4 More Stories Pack A

April *Superdog*, Stage 9 Magpies

May *Green Island*, Stage 9 Magpies

June *In the Garden*, Stage 6 Owls

July *The treasure chest*, Stage 6 Owls

August *The water fight*, Stage 2 More Stories Pack A

September *At school*, Stage1

October *Book week*, Stage 3 More Stories Pack B

November *The storm*, Stage 4

December *Hamid does his best*, Stage 9 More Robins

Oxford University Press, Great Clarendon Street, Oxford OX2 6DP

Oxford New York
Athens Auckland Bangkok Bogota Bombay
Buenos Aires Calcutta Cape Town Dar es Salaam
Delhi Florence Hong Kong Istanbul Karachi
Kuala Lumpur Madras Madrid Melbourne
Mexico City Nairobi Paris Singapore
Taipei Tokyo Toronto Warsaw

and associated companies in
Berlin Ibadan

Oxford is a trade mark of Oxford University Press

© Oxford University Press 1998
First published 1998

ISBN 0 19 838222 7

Typeset and designed by Oxprint Design, Oxford

Printed in Hong Kong